BWB Texts

Short books on big subjects from great New Zealand writers

Playing for Both Sides

Love Across the Tasman

STEPHANIE JOHNSON

To Rosie Scott

Published in 2016 by Bridget Williams Books Limited, PO Box 12474, Wellington 6144, New Zealand, www.bwb.co.nz, info@bwb.co.nz.

ISBN 9780947492991 (Paperback), ISBN 9780947492267 (EPUB)
ISBN 9780908321698 (KINDLE), ISBN 9780908321704 (PDF)
ISTC A02201600000000C5
DOI 10.7810/9780947492991

A catalogue record for this book is available from the National Library of New Zealand. Kei te pātenga raraunga o Te Puna Mātauranga o Aotearoa te whakarārangi o tēnei pukapuka

Acknowledgements
The publisher acknowledges the ongoing support provided by the Bridget Williams Books Publishing Trust and Creative New Zealand.

creative nz
ARTS COUNCIL OF NEW ZEALAND TOI AOTEAROA

Publisher: Tom Rennie
Editors: Geoff Walker and Jane Parkin
Cover and internal design: Base Two
Typesetter: Tina Delceg
Printer: Printlink, Wellington

CONTENTS

INTRODUCTION

In three weeks I will join my Australian-born, New Zealand-raised son, the singer/songwriter Skyscraper Stan, on part of his solo tour of Australia. July and early August 2015 he is playing Sydney, Brisbane, the Gold Coast and Byron Bay, before flying to Perth and Darwin. I'll leave the tour the day before he and his manager go on to Perth.

It was his suggestion that I join him for his mid-July birthday in Sydney and then carry on up the coast as far as Brisbane. I'm to be Roadie Ma.

This little book is an account of that tour, as well as a kind of memoir about my relationship with Australia, a country that has loomed large in my life, as it has in the lives of many New Zealanders.

A friend once told me a story about an elderly man in a nursing home. He has dementia and doesn't know where he is. He thinks he's in Australia. He rings up his wife and tells her, 'Don't come to Australia. It's horrible here.'

Ever since I heard that story I've wondered about the old man's past. Is it just some quirk of the failing brain that he thinks he's in Australia, because he spends hours in front of the television being barked at by Australian ads and watching *Neighbours*? Or has he spent a life going back and forth across the Tasman, like many of us, and now can't quite fathom where he's ended up?

ONE

I

In July 2016 I will take up the Randell Residency in Wellington and begin work on a social history called *West Island,* about the lives in Australia of writer and communist Jean Devanny; painter Roland Wakelin; poet, playwright and editor Douglas Stewart; journalist and right-wing agitator Eric Baume; and writer and bon vivant Dulcie Deamer. The book will tell the stories of these five colourful early to mid-twentieth-century New Zealanders who, instead of swapping the South Island for the North or the city for the country, went west. Throughout their transplanted lives, most maintained a strong sense of being New Zealanders, even though they were all first-generation Pākehā. None of them returned to live:

Australia provided what New Zealand for various reasons did not. It was where they settled and had careers and families, where they made their lives meaningful, where it was easier (or harder) to get by. Their forebears had not been in New Zealand for long enough to form a sense of really belonging, yet these children of immigrants who themselves left our shores felt themselves somehow intrinsically different from white Australians.

In her autobiography, Jean Devanny, who arrived in Sydney in 1929, recalls how she and her husband marvelled to find Sydneysiders so 'foreign':

> Many of the social aspects of Sydney shocked us. For instance, the ramifications of the White Australia Policy. All enlightened New Zealanders of my generation detested the White Australia Policy. The teaching of pride in, and respect for, our native people the Maoris was part of the school curriculum ... the New Zealand Labour Movement had reflected this feeling. It had officially pronounced the WAP to be a nefarious and reactionary doctrine ...'[1]

Although the policy is long gone and barely remembered as an unfortunate chapter in Australian history – overwhelmed perhaps by the more recent heartbreak over the Stolen Generation – the lack of respect for indigenous people still shocks many young New Zealanders when they make their trip across the Tasman. New Zealanders of Māori descent typically encounter open expressions of racial discrimination. In the summer of 2011–12, I lived for a brief period in the hinterlands of Byron Bay. One afternoon I heard on local radio a report about a riot that had taken place in a Queensland secondary school that was apparently started by New Zealanders. The reporter, urged on by the host, eventually conceded that the culprits were Maoris [*sic*]. No explanation was given as to what provocation the New Zealanders had received before they reacted violently. Sadly, it is easy to imagine the taunts and jibes that likely met their young ears.

Over the past few years, Australia has received a bad press in New Zealand, and not only for behaviour on the cricket field. First there were stories of resident New Zealand children being denied medical care and higher education. More recently, many of us were horrified by the detainment of New Zealanders in Villawood and Christmas Island. Some of these men were criminals; many were not, including former Lance Corporal Ngati Kanohi Te Eke Haapu. Otherwise known as Ko, this young New Zealander has committed no crime at all and, at the time of writing (January 2016), has been held in a maximum-security prison for four months. He came to the attention of the authorities by visiting a friend from the Rebels – a motorcycle gang with which he was loosely affiliated – who is detained in Casuarina in Perth. Outside the prison Ko was grabbed and flung into a cell, where he has languished ever since. He has no idea when he will be released.

The Australian rationale for his incarceration is a law passed in 2014 designed to crack down on foreign immigrants of 'character'. The arrest of this soldier, who fought alongside the Australians in Afghanistan, suggests that the ANZAC spirit is mighty sick. Our Prime Minister, for whom Ko once acted as bodyguard in Afghanistan, has not at the time of writing intervened on his behalf.

Despite these distressing signs of tearing in the trans-Tasman relationship, many of us continue to have close personal relationships with West Island. Even after the recent wave of returning disgruntled Kiwis, an estimated 650,000 New Zealanders currently make their home there. Many families are as bifurcated as mine is – not only does my adult son live there, but also my husband's family and many of our friends.

Most of my twenties were spent in Sydney, with my first books bearing on the dust jacket: 'Stephanie Johnson is a young Australian writer'. My own people have been in New Zealand since the 1840s – longer than any of the proposed five subjects for *West Island* – yet I was happy to let the untruth stand for reasons that are complex and some of them hardly honourable. But then, who believes in nationalism any more, really? Weren't those of us born in the sixties taught as five-year-olds to sing the song that imagined there are no countries and nothing to kill or die for? And 'Kookaburra Sits in the Old Gum Tree' and 'Waltzing Matilda'? We sang them as our own songs and knew more about Henry Lawson than we did about Thomas Bracken.

Last October I made a trip to further my research into the life of Douglas Stewart. Born in Eltham, Taranaki, in 1913, Stewart went to live in Sydney in the mid-thirties and never returned to New Zealand to live. He is remembered now as a major twentieth-century Australian poet, essayist and short story writer. For over forty years he edited the 'Red Page', the literary section of the famous *Bulletin* magazine. In that capacity, and also later as an editor for publishers Angus & Robertson, he nurtured and encouraged younger writers on both sides of the Tasman, including Eve Langley, James K. Baxter and Vincent O'Sullivan.

In Sydney, the night before I started reading Stewart's correspondence in the Mitchell Library, I had a dream that stayed with me long enough for me to write it down: *I am in a dark auditorium, like a mall cinema, brown, with a low sloping raised area along one side. A group of young boys on the side stage do a haka. Somebody announces we are going to sing the New Zealand anthem. The music starts and I begin singing – but it's the Australian anthem. I burst out laughing, alone in the crowd apart from one of the haka boys, who catches my eye. Then the music starts for the New Zealand one, but no one except me and a little boy next to me know the words.*

If I had had this dream during the Commonwealth Games, its source could have been constant exposure to 'Australians let us all rejoice for we are young and free!' as the green and gold won medal after medal. 'I'm so sick of the Australian national anthem!' is a common Kiwi complaint during the Games. Since there were no major sporting events at the time, I suppose the dream could be seen as evidence of preoccupation with nationalism, a dream born of an anxiety that I don't really experience in my day-to-day life. It's true that my return home in 1989 felt premature, but I believed at the time we had made the decision for the right reasons: namely baby Stan, for whom we thought we could make a better life in my hometown of Auckland.

For several years after our return, I had the eerie feeling that my Sydney life continued, that I had somehow split in half and lived two lives at once; I had only to somehow find the money for a plane fare and I could slip back inside that other skin. In Auckland I missed the upbeat, coarse, devil-may-care attitude Australians pride themselves on, their desire to laugh at anything, as well as the sense that Australia was somehow more international, more a part of the world than we were. The occasional parochialism of fellow New Zealand writers depressed me, and never more so than when I was asked by a well-known male writer at a friend's book launch, 'Who did you sleep with to get your books published in England?' An Australian writer may well have asked the same question of a young woman, but more likely as a bad joke. This was said with real vitriol, an unwillingness to share in rare success: the truth is, very few books by New Zealanders are published outside our country.

The longing to return waxed and waned, and still does on the rare occasion. When my 1998 novel *The Whistler* was shortlisted for an Australian science-fiction prize, the organisers contacted me to check that I was Australian and only domiciled in New Zealand. 'I'm a sixth-generation New Zealander!' I said proudly, and was immediately disqualified for having the wrong passport. I wondered then, why didn't I stay? When I see the much larger advances Australian writers receive, I can't help but wonder, why am I still here?

When I go to Sydney to research in the Mitchell Library (which, as it happens, contains a fair bit of our literary and historical taonga) I think, why don't I live here? When I travel through infinite forests of gums, or follow a horizon of broken, ancient mountains, or walk among a colony of gentle wallabies on a wild beach, I long to have that land at my doorstep always. I don't remember making a clear decision to stay in New Zealand, but that is what has happened and it seems likely that I'll live here for the rest of my life.

My husband Tim is Australian. He fell in love with New Zealand and has not ever really longed to return to Australia permanently. Our daughters Maeve and Willa were born here, in a house just around the corner from where I am writing now. Maeve is one of the thousands of young New Zealanders to return from Australia in the past couple of years, the exodus stemmed. She is twenty-five and may well go back again – and if she does it would be with my blessing, not that she needs it. Like many parents who worry that our little country will not provide a secure enough future for our adult kids, I find myself obsessing about how low our wages are, how scarce the opportunities to make a living wage, how sad it is our unions are so decimated, how tragic it is that the left is so demoralised and that the voting public is in love with uncaring neo-liberals. But that is pretty much the same all over the west.

Maeve is the same age I was when I left for the first time. It seems to me now that the New Zealand I left was a kind of paradise.

II

In 1985 I flew to Sydney at the invitation of a Kiwi erstwhile boyfriend who had come back to New Zealand briefly with short-lived declarations of undying love. It was the first time I had ever left my homeland.

Until my departure, Australia had held little fascination for me – apart from being the subject of a childhood poem written for a primary school Social Studies project:

> On we go, through and through
> Past koala and kangaroo
> The long-legged emu cries out 'I see you
> and you look just as strange as I!'
> Soon so soon we run out of peas
> We'll have to go and ask the Aborigines ...

The rest of the poem, perhaps luckily, I can't remember.

My father's brother, a successful businessman, made many trips to Australia through the sixties and seventies, and would bring back presents for my siblings and me – koalas of varying sizes made from kangaroo fur, a kangaroo-skin purse that I treasured for years, as well as American and English toys not available in New Zealand. It's likely, though not certain, the purse was made from the scrotal sack of a buck kangaroo. I didn't know this at the time and I don't suppose Uncle Doug did either.

For a short time during my childhood, we had a living Australian amongst us in the shape of a small green budgerigar. My Great-Uncle Eric, a stalwart of the Social Credit Party and breeder of goats in Greenhithe, had for a time an Australian girlfriend. In 1971, when I emerged from Middlemore Hospital after yet another protracted recovery from orthopaedic surgery, the girlfriend gave me Bobby, who spoke with an Australian accent. 'Geedoiy Steefnoie,' he said. In our house Bobby learned to speak with a New Zealand accent, and he also learned to say 'Shut your head!', to yell for my brother to get out of bed for his breakfast and for someone to answer the phone. When I practised my cello he would scream at the top of his voice. On sunny days his cage was hung on a hook on the veranda so that he could 'talk to the other birds'. One winter evening I forgot to bring him inside and he died of cold. It was the first and only time I have been responsible for the death of a pet, and among the many creatures I have loved and nurtured through my life there has never been another caged bird. The overwhelming feeling I have when observing the plumage or clever chat of a feathered prisoner is one of sadness.

This avuncular and avian evidence of another country so near and so different didn't pique my interest enough to want to go there. I was more curious about the lands of my long-ago forebears, the countries that featured in the playground game of elastics: England, Ireland, Scotland, Wales, inside, outside, puppy dog tails! Like most New Zealanders of my generation fortunate enough to belong to a library, I grew up on Brothers Grimm fairy tales, on Beatrix Potter and Enid Blyton, Elizabeth Goudge and John Townsend, Roald Dahl, the Brontës, Oscar Wilde, Charles Dickens and D. H. Lawrence – all of whom reflected back a country that was very like home but wasn't. It was enviably different, somehow superior. The new radio station Hauraki played bands from Great Britain; the music I played on the piano and cello came from Europe, which was near England, wasn't it?

As a little girl I desperately wanted to be English or Irish or Scottish, to be more 'real'. A conversation I remember very clearly, from when I was about eight years old, happened while I was travelling over the Auckland Harbour Bridge with my grandparents en route to our modest three-generation family bach at Torbay, then still rural. I asked my grandmother what we were. 'We're British,' she said firmly, though she was herself second-generation white Fijian. I was relieved. Perhaps I really could have the adventures of the Secret Seven or the Famous Five. Perhaps I really could wake up one morning and see a unicorn in our garden or witness a little swallow plucking the jewelled eyes from a statue.

But I wasn't to go to England until my late thirties. Australia was the country I went to and stayed in for several years, and it is the only country apart from New Zealand in which I have lived for more than a few months. Europe, even after I had had novels published in England, was not to be visited for another fourteen years as a side-trip from France when I was the Katherine Mansfield Fellow, by which time I had an Australian husband and three children.

Youthful love affairs are to some degree imaginary – we fall in love with what we know of a man or woman and imagine the rest, which in many cases is glorious, super-human. That way disappointment surely lies. My returning boyfriend had left to seek his fortune as a cameraman. There were no film schools in New Zealand then, and through our tumultuous years together he had worked on films and television as a clapper loader or grip. The first time I ever heard those terms I loved them immediately. They were hilarious. Later, as we tore one another apart and I weathered his bits-on-the-side, I came to think of the job descriptions as more descriptive of the man himself. But all that lay ahead.

He'd been gone for over a year and we had finally, I thought, split some months before that. He was my first true love; I loved the bones of him, heart and soul. He was from a small regional North Island city, slight and graceful, shone with health and curiosity, read widely, talked incessantly and could play the guitar. At the time we met, one afternoon in the Canterbury University library, he was finishing his degree in clinical psychology. We were nineteen and twenty-one, and I think it was love at first sight. We shared a textbook for an arts paper and I remember his hands on the page – beautiful, long hands that were larger than my freakishly giant ones.

I had been a very lucky girl, sent by my hard-working father to one of Auckland's most expensive girls' secondary schools, which, though it may not mean to, fosters in many of us a life-long delight in the exclusive company of women. In the time since the clapper loader and I had split, I had slid very happily back into a world that at first glance was similar. It was exciting intellectually, politically and sexually – my first love at eleven was a girl, and there had been a couple of adult attachments since then. It wasn't long before I fell in love with a softly spoken, clever gentlewoman from America.

In the early eighties, New Zealand was in the grip of fervent feminism. Men, it seemed, were responsible for the parlous state of the environment, endemic violence and child abuse, and it was best to stay away from them. There was a worldwide movement against pornography, which had resulted in an uncomfortable alliance between right wingers, Christians and feminists, and I had written a play, *Accidental Phantasies*, about the issue. In it women played men, a fairly novel idea at the time, though Caryl Churchill had done it before me (in England, of course), and it was very funny. Or at least, the first act was. At the opening night in Wellington the audience was in stitches, watching Chips in his diner on the Desert Road welcome a group of disparate travellers, all of whom seemed to know something about a car crash up the road. It was rude and sexy. The second act was the car crash itself and this is where the play fell apart. Didactic, preachy, boring – Hugh Hefner and the Marquis de Sade came face to face with Eve, a character based on Jennifer Beard, the victim of a high-profile disappearance in the seventies.

In the time since the clapper loader had departed for the sunburnt country, I had lived in a couple of houses full of musicians, actors, drifters and sensible women who had sensible jobs. I was already establishing what was to be a pattern of feast or famine, working as an actress (we said 'actress' proudly in those days, being mindful of how many centuries it had taken us to get on the stage in the first place) and writing plays and film scripts, sometimes for money.

There were employment schemes, PEP schemes – they seem quaint now in their concern for giving young people an occupation – and the result was a grassroots training for actors, writers and musicians, many of whom have gone on to have successful careers. No doubt the schemes could be another reason for the current beleaguered generations to resent the baby boomers (we were at the tail end of the demographic spike) – this evidence of a caring society, presided over by one Robert Muldoon. From this distance, Muldoon's politics seem bizarrely conflicted – he was at once dictatorial but oddly socialist. He will forever earn the ire of those of us on the left for his immediate dismantling of the New Zealand Superannuation Scheme in 1975, which by conservative estimates would be worth over 300 billion today. His Think Big plans for mining and industry were controversial; he brought Australia to the fore in the thinking of many with his 1982 free trade agreement with that country, the CER, or Closer Economic Relations. But at least his generation of politician seemed to understand the concept that they were the people's servants, not bumboys for international corporations. He was old-style National Party – protectionist, fiercely patriotic and still concerned enough for the little man (and woman) to try to make it easier for us, now and again, on a rare occasion.

Life in Auckland was, on the surface, pretty full and blissful. There was lots of laughter, wild parties and righteous anger – the soon-to-be-victorious anti-nuke movement was in full flower. We angsted about acid rain, overpopulation, and sexism, lookism and ageism. I was to write about this time with satirical affection in my 2001 novel *The Shag Incident*. My third play was in rehearsal, I had published some short stories and poetry, I was a regular at the Globe readings where I hobnobbed with all manner of poets and poetesses (yes). I was a founding member of the Women's Political Party. I remember sitting upstairs at Espresso Love, a popular long-gone café in Three Lamps in Ponsonby, and looking out towards the blue Waitakeres and thinking I was at the centre of the world. I never gave a thought to leaving the country. The closest I got to thinking about the future was one winter night after leaving the Open Late Café on the corner of Richmond Road. I looked up at the clear starry sky and made a private, solemn vow that given the ruined state of the environment I must never ever ever ever have children – how could I bring them into this pre-Apocalypse?

One afternoon in 1985, I was single again and visiting my parents when my flatmate rang to tell me that my old boyfriend was in town and was looking for me. The news was not only puzzling but alarming – what could he possibly want?

Children of the sixties, as in children actually born in the decade and not the older baby boomers who hold the banner, were enormously influenced by that earlier generation. To be 'different' was aspirational; to have 'experiences' was a method for living. The first sat uneasily with me – I was a buck-toothed lippy half-crippled skinny girl who wished desperately to be normal. When my primary school began afternoon ballet classes in the hall, I insisted that my mother take me along. Of course I could do none of the things that were required, not even the skipping, having one leg shorter than the other, and sore, malformed feet barely responding to seven or eight lengthy operations so far. My disappointing appearance in the long mirror and the reflected sympathetic glances of other mothers made me furious and sad. I hated being pitied. In the same vein, after the Paradise Rink opened in Avondale when I was about fourteen, I decided I would take up ice-skating. Only a trip to Mr King the orthopaedic surgeon would dissuade me. It was as if I thought sheer willpower would make me 'normal'. When I read in our ancient Arthur Mee's *The Children's Encyclopaedia* that wild birds will peck to death birds of brighter plumage released from a cage (the reason I would not set Bobby free, though my hand rested often enough on the wire door as he hung on his outside hook), it made perfect sense to me. Of course they would. Nature's way and no use wishing. But why would you want to be different if you weren't? It was a puzzle.

In some of us, the legacy of disability and its good friend the playground bully is an almost pathological desire to please, to enter an apologetic state for being so wrong, to try to revert to normalcy. Or is it reversion? It may as easily be that we go forward to it, climb the slope and struggle to triumph on the peak of general acceptance.

I left my parents' house in a familiar emotional state: a sense of cleaving, a bifurcation of my self. It was how I could pass in the able-bodied world as one of them – I was an actress, wasn't I, of sorts? – and how I could pass just as easily between lesbian and heterosexual groups of friends, though less and less, since the transition filled me with guilt of almost religious acuity. *People are the same everywhere* ran a piece of common wisdom handed out in the sixties, intended to comfort. Far from *celebrating difference*, as we try to today, the ideal was a smooth, homogeneous society. By the 1980s, it was very clear that we weren't the same. There were very real divisions between people, to do with ability, religion, race, class, sexuality and culture, and they were becoming more apparent every day. I seemed to be either ignorant of them or painfully aware.

How would my erstwhile boyfriend see me, as I was now?

I went home, he came round, but only flashes of our reunion remain in my memory. I can see him arriving, walking smiling down the sunny autumn path of my flat. I remember how he took me in his arms and how there was a hunger in him for me that didn't seem to have any connection to who I actually was. It set off dimly ringing (dinner?) bells – *this isn't real* – but suddenly I wanted it to be. I wanted to be beside him again. He had been halfway around the world, he told me, and had never met anyone like me. I would love Sydney; he wanted me to go back with him. He sniffed the nape of my neck. 'You still smell the same.' He loved me. I was confused.

Another memory – sitting on a low windowsill, a hot window behind me, the sound of the sea and the sun glancing off a cork-tiled floor (we must have gone away somewhere together, he and I, although I can't remember where), and hearing myself tell him I was a lesbian now and couldn't live with him, but that I would come to Australia. I remember how disappointed he seemed but how quickly he covered it with his usual tough humour. And also I had to wait until *Accidental Phantasies* opened at the Depot in Wellington, with its fabulous cast that included Lorae Parry (Chips/Priest), May Lloyd (the Truckie/Eve) and

Fiona Samuel (Andy/Hugh Hefner), and that was a month or so off.

Restored to me body and soul, my beloved went back to Sydney. I was familiar again with the urgent longing for him, the gap he left in my life. I went to Wellington, attended the opening night in a tuxedo and bow tie, and was so pissed and overwhelmed that when the audience called 'Author! Author!', no doubt in relief at having survived the second act, I had to be supported between two kind friends who also straightened my bow tie.

Home to Auckland for two days and a going-away party. It was a scandal. I had a lesbian going-away party and I was 'going back to men'. I protested feebly – no, only one man. A woman I barely knew suggested that since I was going to be doing it with him, I may as well do it with lots of others and get paid for it. Most friends, particularly older friends, were kind and understanding. There was a generational divide between older and younger – those who called themselves children of the sixties eschewed labels; the true children of the sixties embraced them with fervour. Murky sexual identities were shameful.

My bricklayer Pop had died recently and left me a little hard-earned money that was enough to get me started across the Tasman. My cello and I departed, and took all my confusion with us.

III

At the airport I was met by the clapper loader in a big white camera van, and on the way into the city he told me in colourful language how he'd slept with a girl the night before and no matter how much strident effort he put into the exercise he was deprived of an orgasm. I was stunned. I thought we were reunited with dry cheeks, like the Emmylou Harris song. But 'possessiveness' is wrong, isn't it? (Our generation would ask one another earnestly 'Are you possessive?' just as we would ask 'Are you ambitious?' Both were negative qualities.)

Then he asked me why I had on so much make-up. I hadn't worn street make-up for years and had forgotten how to do it, if I ever knew. 'You're not a dollybird. You look stupid.'

As I wept copiously at his betrayal, my pancake melted, mascara ran, lurid green eyeshadow slipped, and my eyes stung and swelled as if they were poisoned. We drove in silence to a terraced house in Yurong Street, Darlinghurst, which was full of dust-rimmed artefacts collected by his landlord/flatmate from native peoples of New Guinea and Indonesia. Our bedroom was an entirely windowless upstairs room empty of masks and figurines, with thick fetid-smelling shagpile carpet, nanna-ish gold and white wallpaper, his guitar, a ghetto blaster and a mattress on the floor.

As the weeks went by I would wake in the morning and think overly dramatic thoughts like 'I am in enemy territory', especially after nights spent with Australians who were so vastly different from the New Zealanders I'd left behind. Sexist, derogatory remarks were manifold, as were racist ones ('You're so lucky to have the Maoris', usually said by Australians unhappy with the 'Aboriginal situation'), and I wasn't sure it was cool for the landlord to have so many native artefacts. Our room was pitch black with the door closed. In the mornings we would reach for one another, and for a little while everything would be roses again.

Then during the day, while he clapped and loaded, I wandered around as far as my feet would carry me, with long, painful rests, searching for peace in the beauty of Hyde Park or Mrs Macquarie's Chair or St Mary's Cathedral. Sydney was beautiful, though frightening. I fell in love with the new quality of light, with swimming at Nielsen Park in the deep, rocky harbour with water the colour of kerosene (on the map the beach is marked 'Shark Bay'), a harbour so different from the muddy, tidal Waitematā. I loved the old sandstone buildings and the hints of the convict past. There were lizard-headed ibis, raucous cockatoos, rosellas and kookaburras, and I thought how lucky Sydneysiders were that their native birds had adjusted better to city life than ours had. The flying foxes that rose at dusk from the Morton Bay fig trees in the Botanic Gardens were a fairy tale. On a trip away to a farm in the New England tablelands, I swam in a creek and a magical platypus went past in a stream of bubbles.

But I was scared. I didn't know who I was any more. I suspected I had made a big mistake but knew also that when we were good together you couldn't have better. We would have giggling attacks like kids. We would lie close and listen to one another's thoughts ear to ear, or to his collection of cassettes – Keith Jarrett, Phoebe Snow, Joni Mitchell, Eric Clapton, J. J. Cale – touchstone music that went some way to stilling the clamour in my head.

It wasn't long before I discovered that the best cure for the clamour, as writers have known from the time humans first put chisel to stone, is to write. In New Zealand I had written poetry and plays, and had often been in the company of thespians. In Sydney I knew no one except the cameraman, and my disability meant I could not do the usual waitressing/bar jobs young New Zealanders take up – jobs that provide both money and new friends. I had one attempt as a dishwasher and couldn't walk for days afterwards. I started to write prose, short stories and my first novel, absorbing myself in fictional worlds so that I didn't have to fret about the real one. It was wonderfully liberating – no longer did I have to think about cast sizes, or how to tell a story limited to bodies and voices in a room, helped only by lighting and costuming. I remember a sense of exhilarating freedom – anything was possible. A character could walk upside down on a ceiling; a crowd scene wouldn't blow the budget.

I had to work against the instinctive self-doubt that I believe plagues many New Zealanders, particularly of the post-war generations. We are quick to put ourselves down, slow to believe in ourselves, tempted to dwell on the negative. All I knew was that writing gave me enormous pleasure and comfort, just as reading always had, and that it was pretty much all I wanted to do and it was surprisingly similar. I had always been a storyteller to my younger siblings and cousins – the dramas would unfurl, the scenes play out in my mind's eye. My first novel *Crimes of Neglect*, set around Darlinghurst and the Cross, began to take shape in my mind.

The clapper loader (now promoted to focus puller) and I moved to another house in Surry Hills. My small stash of money was running out rapidly, even though I eschewed normal human activities like eating. I would ring up about jobs I saw advertised in the *Sydney Morning Herald* or the *Trading Post*. One was for a receptionist for a private eye. This sounded like the dream job.

'You're a New Zealander, aren't ya?' he asked, early on in the convo. 'Look, love – your countrywomen have done you a great disservice. I've had two or three New Zealand housekeepers and they just cleaned me out. Left me with nothing. I belong to Rotary and a few organisations like that – businessmen, you know – and none of us will employ New Zealanders.'

I wondered if they'd signed a pact.

'Maori girls. The housekeepers.'

'I'm not Maori.' The words were out of my mouth before I thought further. I was consumed with guilt. I was appealing to his racist instincts.

'Doesn't matter,' he said. 'You're all the same.' He hung up.

It was my first real experience of brazen racial discrimination and I was entirely unprepared for it. Of course there were all the jokes. (An Australian, an American and a New Zealander are on a sinking life raft. Grab anything we don't need and chuck it over, says the American. So the Australian throws the New Zealander into the sea. How do you pick the New Zealander in the shoe shop? He's the one trying on the boxes.)

My daughter Maeve says she never heard any jokes like these in her five years in Melbourne, and we wonder whether that's generational or the enduring difference between the two cities. Melbourne is the current go-to city in Australia for young New Zealanders, and mostly they seem to enjoy a level of respect and trust.

Most of the jokes, and they were legion, were internationally interchangeable, just as likely to be bigotry about the Irish/Blacks/mothers-in-law/blondes. The best jokes I knew in response to a laconic wisecracker were pretty pathetic. (Why do seagulls fly upside down over Manly? Because Australians aren't worth shitting on. How many Australians does it take to change the kitchen light bulb? None – let the beetch cook in the dark.)

I made a brief return trip to New Zealand to collect the Bruce Mason Memorial Playwrights Award, arriving in arctic Wellington in an orange singlet and inch-long hair. I was graceless at the award ceremony, never having attended anything like it and not knowing a speech was required. I bumbled around Wellington, bewildered. A strong gust of wind blew my 44-kilo self through an orange safety barrier and into a hole on Lambton Quay. Bruised and bronchial, I returned to Sydney, where I felt more at home, or warmer, at least, and was very glad of the generosity of the award. I felt guilty, though. Was I obliged to go home, since I had won the prize?

During those first months in Sydney, I had already heard tell of the Kiwi ghetto, which was supposed to centre on Bondi. There, since the fifties, New Zealanders had occupied brick-and-tile flats, grotty rooms above shops and rooming houses. They'd partied, surfed, misbehaved and earned an unfortunate reputation for living off the Aussie dole (for which we continued to be eligible until Prime Ministers John Howard and Helen Clark came to an agreement in 2001). Although I never lived in Bondi and never went surfing, for a short time I fulfilled the other criteria for becoming the classic Kiwi bludger.

Eventually I landed a job as assistant in the news-clipping library of the ABC at Artarmon, and life came into some sort of balance. Self-esteem is difficult to hold on to at any stage of life and more so when you're young – mine was zero. But I was setting off each day on the train to the North Shore and earning some money, and was able to see the road ahead a little more clearly. The focus puller and I found the strength finally to end our disastrous relationship and I moved out, firstly to the Cross to stay with a New Zealand friend, and then into a succession of flats.

During the following year, I was taken on by Cameron's Agents and was cast in *Dogs in Space,* Richard Lowenstein's semi-autobiographical film shot in Melbourne. I play Erica, who wears a pink boilersuit and tries unsuccessfully to take off with Michael Hutchence's girlfriend. In preparation for the role I studied hard to gain an Australian accent. I wanted one anyway, to stem the wearisome tide of sheep and bludger jokes. The accent took root. Even now, after nearly three decades back home, it will leap out at inopportune moments and overwhelm my native vowels, particularly if I am nervous. It's embarrassing, especially if it happens during an interview or public speech.

With my freshly minted Australian accent I returned to Sydney, where Cameron's literary arm represented me on my first book of short stories, *The Glass Whittler*. And on the dust jacket of the Australian edition I was claimed as one of their own.

By this stage I had moved into a shared house in Centennial Park with a group of young Aussies who had advertised for a female flatmate. One of them was an editor at the ABC, a curly-haired, blue-eyed, immediately loveable man called Tim. He loved poetry and music and could speak Spanish, he was a man of the world and, despite my broken foot (I had fallen down some stairs in my last grotty flat) and general insolvency, he fell in love with me. I'm sure that many times in our thirty years together he has regretted his impulsive heart. I was slow to trust again, slow to believe that love could be truly, madly, deeply – but love did bloom and we have been together ever since. He is the father of my children, my very best friend in all the world, and tomorrow I will say goodbye, see you in two weeks, I'm going west to see our lad.

TWO

The Tour

14 July

On the plane to Sydney I have a little girl beside me, perhaps seven or eight years old. From the moment she takes her seat she is hooked into the seatback screen. She has a supply of jelly snakes and jabs at the controls with increasingly sticky fingers. On the other side of the aisle sit her mother and younger sister. The mother looks tired. The little sister is demanding of attention and the mother seems to have her on her lap whenever the seat belt sign is turned off. The older sister eats her store of sweets and watches her in-flight entertainment and I worry about how stultifying to the human brain the diet of sugar and screens is – though unlike neighbouring children she doesn't divide her attention between a bright iPad on her lap and images on the seatback. Like me, the little family have bought cheap seats – no meal, no movies – so she's watching reruns of TVNZ, paying particular attention to an episode of *The Zoo*.

As we begin our descent, the shadowy coast of New South Wales spreading north in the sunset, the little girl tries to get her mother's attention. Eventually the younger sister is ignored for long enough for the elder to say her piece, which is to do with Anjalee, the new elephant at Auckland Zoo. It is a detailed, humorous, well-constructed little observation and the mother laughs. The daughter is delighted with the response and I think of how it's commonly believed that first children (such as myself and my son) can be more articulate because of all the attention they receive as babies.

Listening to my small fellow passenger, it occurs to me that it may be that our language skills evolve more out of a desire to draw our mother's attention away from the younger ones, traditionally two or three years younger, who are of course cuter and more needful of her focus. If they're grizzly and demanding, then it's up to number one to give Mum a distraction or, better still, a laugh. It can be an uphill road, and uphill roads are something my firstborn knows more than I would have hoped for him.

Sydney is having an uncharacteristically cold snap, but a small crowd has ventured out to the

Golden Cinema bar in Surry Hills, a central-city suburb. As I cross the narrow street towards the venue I can hear the strains of Stan's voice and guitar. For a moment I pause to look through the street-level window into the basement room where he sings on a mirrored stage. No one except his girlfriend is listening. The others are far more interested in whatever they have to say to one another than in listening to a tall skinny dude singing his heart out.

He acknowledges me as I enter the bar – there's my mother, just off the plane from New Zealand. The crowd gives him a moment of attention and my appearance a smattering of applause. The same pride that always fills me when I hear him sing does so again, but battles with irritation with the constant talkers. He seems impossibly thinner, his clothes more worn, his boots scuffed and holed. A woman at a table near the front sits with her back to him and only stops talking to stuff chips in her gob.

A man beside me tells me he heard Stan sing in Melbourne and comes to hear him in Sydney whenever he can. He says he tells his friends – see him before you have to pay fifty bucks. I think how I can't wait for that day to arrive. The man asks me – how did you feel when he told you he wanted to be a musician? I tell him: he was one of those kids who could have done anything. This is an exaggeration. He would never have made an All

Black or a heavyweight boxer because he's a 6-foot 5-and-a-half and a long drink of water; or a soldier or a policeman because he's a free spirit.

All mothers think their children are brilliant and unique, and just as well for them. My daughters like to tease me about how I love Stan best of all. I don't love him any more than I love them, but I'm pretty astonished by the mere fact of having a son. When he was born I thought of all the poor queens of England and Scotland who had their heads cut off for their inability to provide an heir – and felt smug. For many women a daughter is natural, almost expected. The response to the arrival of a little mate and beloved daughter for life could be 'So there you are, my darling – what took you so long?' A male creature who bears attributes of his mother and, more importantly, of the man she loves is more a shout from the rooftops – 'Would you look at this! He's a bloody miracle!'

16 July

Today the miracle turns twenty-seven years old, which is the age I was when he was born. In her sunny, lofty Glebe flat, my dearest friend Rosie Scott makes us a delicious birthday lunch – sausages, tender little lamb chops, hummus, salad, cheese, eggs, crusty bread and fruit. We laugh and talk the afternoon away. Rosie is a New Zealander who published her first novel, *Glory Days*, in 1988 while still living in Auckland. She and I pretty much crossed paths mid-Tasman – Rosie, her Australian husband Danny Vendramini and two daughters going west, while Tim, Stan and I headed east. Since then she has had a luminary career as writer, mentor, writing teacher and political activist in West Island. She has even gone so far as to take dual New Zealand/Australian citizenship, which I like to rib her about, but it's only because I selfishly wish we still had her in the Land of the Long White Cloud.

For Rosie, the desire to pledge allegiance to the five stars came about not only from a deep need to commit to Australia but also to reflect her true, bifurcated nationality after so many years of living and writing there. She is a much-loved and respected public figure. (Although she doesn't yet know it as we have our birthday lunch, in January 2016 she will be awarded the Order of Australia for Services to Literature as an Author, for Human Rights and Intercultural Understanding.)

Rosie's Australian identity has evolved naturally through the years in West Island. Traitorous though the suggestion is, it would be advantageous for every New Zealand resident in Australia to have immediate Australian citizenship, especially now that our mutually accommodating arrangement has been dismantled. It should be top of the list as we get off the plane. The exodus west ran in varying sizes since the eighties ('Last one to leave turn off the lights' was the gag) through to its apex of nearly 54,000 in a single year, 2012. But it was that 2001 change, under which New Zealanders became expected to pay full taxes without receiving any benefits, that precipitated the current deluge of returnees. Unable to access free medical care or tertiary education for our children, and with the safety net of unemployment and sickness benefits snatched away, we are suddenly foreigners on the same footing as any other immigrant. Our old intimacy is brutally disrupted and dispensed with, precisely at a point in our social history when it is almost expected that antipodean families live both sides of the Tasman. The mean-spirited arrangement is not reciprocal – Australians living among us still have access to our health system and universities, just as they always have. Maybe it fits with the stereotypical differences – we are kinder, more polite and possibly dumber. Come in! Help yourself! Take it all! Going cheap!

With this in mind, it is interesting to reflect that in the sixties and seventies Australia was regarded by many young New Zealand travellers merely as a stepping-stone, a place to earn the money before going on to Europe for our true OE, itself a necessary rite of passage. Trans-Tasman rivalry inspired the common response to a young Kiwi heading west: 'Australia! What would you want to go there for?' Perhaps this will be revived.

In general, I think, New Zealanders are not taken seriously in Australia, even though we occupy the upper echelons of almost any field of endeavour imaginable.

In the evening Stan and I go to hear a country and western band called Not Good with Horses at a small Marrickville bar. Neville the drummer is a charming chap my age, born in Invercargill and raised in Dunedin. He has brothers in Auckland. There's a wistfulness in the way he talks about his native land that is often detectable in expatriates, but perhaps it's just nostalgia for the place of childhood, for the past, not necessarily for the New Zealand of today. Later I think about how the correlation to this nostalgia is the change in confidence and increased levels of happiness, especially among men. There are so many tales about so-and-so, Māori or Pākehā, who has vanished off to Australia and come good. 'He's really come out of himself!' we hear again and again. 'He's so much more confident!' Australia can be a positive influence on New Zealand men.

17 July

I have a meeting in the Cross with a journalist. It's cool and rainy, and the Cross is not its usual crowded, colourful self. One of my subjects for *West Island* is a famous Kings Cross figure, Dulcie Deamer, who was born in Christchurch in 1890 and raised by free-thinking, educated parents. At seventeen she won an Australian short story competition, and this precipitated her early marriage and departure for Sydney. Except for early travels further afield, she was to live and write there for the rest of her life, producing journalism, novels and poetry, half of it unpublished and most of it created in various Kings Cross flats.

She was perhaps better known for her involvement in establishing the Australian Fellowship of Authors (a precursor to the ASA) and for her outrageous behaviour – wearing leopard-skin suits and conducting kissing competitions. Crowned Queen of Bohemia in 1925, she dabbled in the dark arts and was the doyenne of a group of leading Australian writers and artists. It was during the thirties and forties that she came briefly into contact with Jean Devanny and Eric Baume, neither of whom liked her much. A selfish narcissist, she was mother to six children, whom she abandoned to the care of their grandmother, and did her best to live the life of Riley. The Cross was a tough place in those days, scruffier and wilder, not the gentrified strip it is today. Louis Nowra's fascinating 2013 book *Kings Cross: A Biography* can be read in part as an elegy to those pre-homogenised days.

The journalist is a very likeable, feisty woman of Irish descent. Her family have been in Australia since the 1840s, as long as mine have been in New

Zealand. She has read my most recent novel *The Writers' Festival*, which she enjoyed, but wonders if it is a little 'too New Zealand'. This is a remark that many Pākehā writers and artists will tell you they hear from Australians. What do they mean, 'too New Zealand'? Would they say 'too Greek' or 'too Korean'?

There is never any point in feeling offended by remarks of this kind. It's important to remember that the (diminishing) ANZAC spirit does not draw us closer: we are different nations, and in Australian eyes we are somehow inferior. There is an idea that the 'too New Zealand' novel or painting will not travel, that our work is somehow inaccessible. This could be a point of pride, or just as easily a cause for great concern. Are we to talk only to ourselves? When I press the journalist about the meaning of her comment, she says it is the place names and the sense of humour. Also, she thinks the central character, Merle, a writing teacher and the author of five novels, has a chip on her shoulder about being a New Zealander. The book was a bestseller of several months' standing at home and no reader or reviewer ever expressed that opinion. I assume she has drawn this conclusion because Merle writes a book set in Australia and sells it there under a pseudonym.

Tangentially, I reflect how interesting it is that the writer subjects I've been researching for *West*

Island rarely paired the two countries in their work. They would set books and stories in either place, and not make comparisons. Critics and biographers, however, would occasionally draw conclusions about the deeper, more far-reaching effects of coming from one country and living in the other. In his 1974 biography *Douglas Stewart,* Clement Semmler remarks:

> It may well be argued that this astonishing versatility may be traced to the fact that Stewart is, or has been, a citizen of two countries – of New Zealand and Australia; and these different backgrounds of experience (and indeed their similarities) have given Stewart a rich storehouse for his literary proclivities, providing him with an extraordinary variety of literary motifs.[2]

Stand by for a tsunami of work from the next generations of writers who straddle the Tasman.

In the afternoon, I meet an older New Zealand friend of Stan's who through the mid- to late twentieth century managed some very famous antipodean rock bands. We talk about the Tuesday-night gig and how nobody listened. Stan calls these gigs 'human jukebox' and has grown a skin thick enough to deal with it. The ex-band manager suggests that if it upsets me to watch him so ignored, then I shouldn't go. In Melbourne, Skyscraper Stan and The Commission Flats were filling pubs and venues, playing to crowds of over a thousand at festivals. Now Stan's taking a break from band wrangling until the summer, taking time to write new songs, so it's back to solo gigging on the road, and smaller, sometimes inattentive audiences. The ex-band manager tells me that in his time there were bands of great promise who couldn't do that backward step necessary to get established in new cities or countries, playing the smaller places – one very well-known lead singer who could have been as big as Jagger spat the dummy in America and got on the next plane home. It was pretty much the end of his international career.

In the early evening Stan sings for an hour in a tiny barbershop in the Cross. The chairs and mirrors are shifted out to make room for the crowd. It's Sydney's coldest day for forty-four years and our breath is frosting. People wending their way home from work stop to listen; a cop car slows on the narrow street to check the gathering crowd, then backs up to catch a song. Two more cops pass on horseback. A couple of people say the same thing as the man at the cinema bar – they heard he was singing for free so they came along.

The crowd is quiet, absorbed, appreciative not just of his music but of the free beers. I'm self-conscious, trying not to have too gormless an adoring expression, as I sit against the wall of the white-tiled shop. When I told friends in New Zealand I was going across to join Stan for the trip north to Queensland, many of them were astonished that a young man would want to share that time with his mother. It astonishes me, too. I'm one lucky mama.

Later that night we are at Lazy Bones in Marrickville, a venue crazily decorated with kitsch and curiosities, a glittery *Kama Sutra* ceiling painting, masses of leather couches and crammed bookcases. A young couple sit reading, holding their books to the light cast by plastic coals. The act tonight is a fantastic ska band. Among its repertoire is a ska version of the famous Māori song 'Hine e Hine', which brings everyone to their feet. The place is heaving with people of all ages and the young drummer has his mother in the audience.

Outside for a cigarette, an old Sydney friend expounds her theory that we are closer to our adult children than our parents were to us, and I wonder why this could be. Because we don't judge them for their precarious lifestyles? Because, even though many of us knew the world was in dire trouble, we brought them guiltily into existence, breaking any promises such as the long-ago one I made outside the Open Late Café?

19 July

Today the news is full of reports of the Reclaim Australia protests across the country. Arrests are being made as the right-wing patriots clash with the rival No Room for Racism groups. In Queensland, a Federal Coalition MP tells the Reclaim Australia rally that Australia is at war with extreme Islam. The opportunities for bigotry seem greater here, particularly since the tragic event in the chocolate shop in Martin Place, at Sydney's heart, in 2014: Man Haron Monis, a rogue gunman with serious mental health issues, took a group hostage and two innocent people lost their lives. The media have made much of other violent crime committed by Muslims, and the internet is choked with anti-Islamic sentiment. In Melbourne a man tattooed with swastikas calls his more thinking opponents 'lefty scum'. There are riots and the police use capsicum spray, separating the crowds by 20 metres.

How sad it all is. I remember a peaceful protest when we wore black armbands and converged in Hyde Park to protest the treatment of Aborigines. It was Australia Day of the Bicentennial Year, 1988, and I was pregnant with Stan. I went into town on the bus on my own and wandered into the park, worried that white people could be unwelcome. The memory of the Bastion Point protest, when we were told by some Ngāti Whātua that the fight wasn't ours, was still fresh. A group of Aboriginal women were seated in a circle on the ground. When they saw me totter by with my big belly they called me over, and I sat with them for the afternoon. It was a sunny day, there were flags and singers and warmth and general acceptance and no violence at all. I heard later that more than 40,000 people had taken part.

21 July

The *Sydney Morning Herald* carries a cartoon of an Aboriginal man addressing a placard-waving Reclaim Australia ocker with a beergut. 'You're about 227 years too late,' the Aboriginal figure is saying.

After a quiet weekend spent with family and Rosie, I'm heading north with Stan and his manager. It's an eleven-hour trip into a brumous, murky night. Like many island dwellers I find myself looking for a glimpse of the sea, but the wide dark roads show none, only industrial areas eventually giving way in the fog to oceanic reaches of eucalypt. Stan's iPod plays male singers. 'You guys don't listen to any chicks,' I observe, to no response. Mostly we talk about the music industry, which runs parallel to the book industry, i.e., it struggles. Young musicians and young writers face the same devil – the triumph of the internet, which is fabulous for promoting work but not for paying out on it. Hand in hand with the conviction that anyone can sing a song or write a novel is the belief that no one should actually part with cash to be so entertained. Spotify, the music-streaming app, has some new demonic cousins such as Scribd and Oyster that stream books. Oyster offers access to over one million books for less than ten dollars a month. Amazon is instigating a new programme for self-published books in which readers pay as they read. How long before they do that to all of us?

We listen to Marlon Williams, a New Zealander making waves in Australia and beloved at home. He has the voice of an angel – unearthly, melancholy. His insightful, beautiful song 'Lonely Side of Her' swoops and lilts; the road opens before us. At Coffs Harbour a sign points to Solitude Park Way. Everything seems to be about loneliness, and I think of the famous quote from American writer Marianne Moore – 'The cure for loneliness is solitude'. It's one I cling to, though I have no need for it tonight. Inside the car it's warm and companionable, we sing and chat.

When we detour briefly off the highway to a country road bordered by tall trees, I worry about the car being blindsided by a kangaroo. (Last time I was in Australia I hit an emu with disastrous results.) The manager makes a joke about how he has an ejector seat specially designed for mothers, so I haul my anxieties in. Young men, it's often remarked, are bullet proof. Recent research goes so far as to suggest that for the optimum development of the male brain it is important that boys indulge in dangerous activities, like climbing mountains and driving fast cars. In the odd way he has of picking up on my thoughts, Stan mentions Nick Cave's teenage son, who had died on the day I arrived in Sydney. The Australian music scene is reeling from the news of his death – he fell from a cliff near their home in England. Nobody wants to think it was suicide and the inquest isn't until November.[3]

We get back onto the highway unmolested by marsupials and cheer ourselves up with more junk food. The highways of Australia are rimmed by service stations, Maccas and Hungry Jacks; the towns with their family-owned cafés are struggling and bypassed. If you want to take a stand against the death-dealing multinational obesity traders, you have to go some distance out of your way.

22 July

Stan plays The Bearded Lady, a funky little bar in Brisbane's West End. There's a small but appreciative audience. A recent reviewer named Stan the best lyricist in Australia – people listen closely, laugh, look delighted. He sings a couple of new rollicking songs, hot off the press. 'Dinnertime at the Poorhouse' has me laughing and crying.

> Well it's breakfast time again down here at the
> poor house
> And you don't know what that means.

Lord I think I'll lose my mind
If I have to eat one more can of beans.
The mice are back in the kitchen again
There's weevil eggs all through the bread.
Hold on boys, I've got a plan
It's all right, it's all right, it's all right.

Now it's lunchtime again down here at the poorhouse
And I'm on the way to my physician
Doctor please this hunger hurts
Worse than a backstreet circumcision.

Well the mice are back in the kitchen again
There's weevil eggs all through the bread.
Hold on boys, I've got a plan
It's all right, it's all right, it's all right.

And I'm creeping down the supermarket aisle
I'm trying hard to hide my guilty smile.
I'm filling my jacket with pretty plastic packets
Then running like it's going out of style.

Well it's dinnertime down here at the poor house
And such a spread is far beyond belief.
You might say I live like a king, I say baby I live
like a thief.

Well the mice are back in the kitchen again
There's weevil eggs all through the bread.
Hold on boys, I've got a plan
It's all right, it's all right, it's all right.
But it's all right Mama, it's all right.

Some far-flung cousins appear, including Henry, who is a budding artist and writes songs and poetry. 'Squash it out of him right now!' I say to his mother, only half-joking, expressing the dilemma of parents of moderate means. Should you be pushing your kids into the professions or encouraging them to sign their lives away to some multinational corporation or borrowing money to set them up in a sandwich bar?

It's interesting to examine the family financial support given to successful musicians. When I was a young cellist, there was a story going around about a certain British cellist of international repute whose father had hired the Royal Albert Hall for his debut concert. My teacher had studied with him and felt he was no better than many, and that his father's wealth had put him on the road to international fame. She was jealous not of his talent but of his luck. Stories like this are manifold – the silverspooners who go to the leading film, theatre and music schools, the kids supported while they seek their fortunes on bigger markets. Cold comfort, but it has always been thus – historically the majority of successful composers and writers came from upper-class families and were supported by the family purse. The starving garret accommodated very few.

All of us in the arts like to believe success – not necessarily stardom, but income enough to provide roof and sustenance – is just around the corner. Contrary to our mad ideas in the eighties, ambition is not a dirty word – it's vital for survival. As a writing teacher I have had the occasional student more set on fame than on anything else, even though the desire to be a famous writer is not necessarily the same as the desire to write. It seems to me that the success in the west of neo-liberal governments is closely connected with this escalation of youthful ambition. The dream these regimes offer is aspirational, one of personal wealth, minimum support of the disadvantaged and an alluring rejection of any proof that our planet is in serious trouble. Our own Prime Minister is a very wealthy man and it seems many voters would far rather strive to emulate his blinkered comfort than adopt the principles of long-forgotten socialists like Mickey Savage. The sad fact is that for most of us the dream of colossal wealth and fame is doomed to failure. Far more achievable is a life lived with an open heart and hard work, holding on to the old ideals of looking to the common good at the same time as having a bit of an adventure when you can. A bit like Mickey Savage, who was, actually, Australian.

23 July

We're waiting at Birkdale train station where a pair of portly cops strut, each openly armed with pistol and Taser, a sight that never fails to alarm

New Zealanders.[4] It is something to be proud of, perhaps, that our police will wear shoulder holsters but mostly keep their weapons in the patrol cars. These cops wear greasy boyish caps, trousers elasticised at the ankle, and multi-pocket vests bulging with notebooks, pens, and possibly cake and sandwiches. Handcuffs, once quaintly called come-alongs, dangle from their belts, and one of them has an iPod stuck into the back of his pants. Both are so overweight it is difficult to imagine them out-running a felon of even limited fitness.

It's three-quarters of an hour into South Bank, and on the journey it seems that Brisbane's three components are sprawling suburbia, swamp and construction sites. Old-style Queenslanders – the wooden houses on poles with shuttered windows – are a rare sight. Like many cities in the New World, Brisbane is meeting its voracious housing demand by spreading to the horizons – it's the fastest-growing city in the country. At South Bank, Stan's namesake skyscrapers puncture the rain clouds, ferries ply to and fro, and a cartoon-style fake beach with white sand and lifeguards has few customers.

Queensland, like New South Wales, is having a record cold winter. Until recently this part of the world enjoyed a monsoonal climate – wet summers and dry winters. This year there have been weeks of heavy rain, and, after the devastating floods of last summer, it is unwelcome and alarming. Perversely, Tony Abbott is in the news for sabotaging solar-energy-sector jobs and axing the Renewable Energy Target. How enviable it is, in some ways, to be so cushioned by wealth and ignorance that the fear of climate change does not touch you. He and our guy are hatched out of the same manky egg kicked to the back of the chookhouse. Abbott's personal fortune has been estimated at AUD$80 million.

Māori artist Lisa Reihana's work 'Venus Infected' is showing in one of the spaces in the Queensland Art Gallery. I've already seen it twice at the Auckland Art Gallery, but I'm happy to sit through it again with Stan. It's a piece of genius – colourful, inspired, generous, wise and playful. Chests puffed out with patriotic pride, we move on to the Australian collection and come across Roland Wakelin's 'The Bridge under Construction' (1928), one of several paintings he made of the building of Sydney Harbour Bridge. I've only ever seen it in reproduction. The real thing is vibrant, surprising – pinks and violets and turquoise.

Wakelin, born in Greytown in 1887, was a revolutionary colour theorist and highly regarded painter, loved not only for his work but for his kindness. In his tribute book, Leslie Walton remarks that Wakelin was a man 'of great inner strength, integrity, straightforwardness of character', that he was 'essentially a generous man with time and money' and sometimes 'mistaken as a little gruff'. I like to think that this was his essential New Zealand character, especially the character of our men of letters and the arts from that generation. 'One always knew where one stood with Wakelin,' writes Walton, 'and the feeling of stability generated a tremendous respect among his family and peers.'[5]

Our integrity, generosity and gruffness – the latter detectable only in the face of loud Aussie hyperbole – are qualities often remarked on across the Tasman. 'You're so ladylike,' Australians would say to me thirty years ago, when ladylikeness was one of my least discernible qualities at home. We have a kind of space around us, I think, a kind of privacy. In the fifties and sixties, they liked to call us South Sea Poms.

Outside the museum is a 10-metre baby brachiosaurus, which wags its tail and makes a kind of mournful muted roar. As I stand with my adult son looking up at it, I'm forcibly reminded of the earnest little boy who loved dinosaurs and had his own 'museum' of treasured fossils and natural artefacts. The Professor, we used to call him. How privileged I am to have this time with him now. I count my blessings.

24 July

We're back on the train again but heading south. Two pistol-packing cops check out the carriage and the senior one makes a gesture for the younger one to follow him out, as if she's a dog. Industrial areas, spreading suburbia, a little bush, and then the canals of the Gold Coast. Stan remarks how the landscape reminds him of New Orleans, where he lived for a period a few years ago – the canals, the low-lying land. It's cold on the surf beach, but tourists are pretending it's warm, parading in bikinis and budgie smugglers. I feel sorry for any New Zealanders who have heeded the ads for a winter break – it's only about 20 degrees. Hotels swanky or grotty, nose-to-tail traffic, shops selling tourist tack (Australia produces so much of it), fast-food venues, clothing chain stores – the same commercial devastation wreaked on the coast up and down.

Stan needs new guitar strings before tonight's gig, so we head along the strip in a streetcar full of Asian tourists carrying bags of shopping – electronic goods, stuffed native-animal toys, boxes of macadamia chocolates. The atmosphere is peaceful, holidaymaking. Perhaps the racist protests have not touched this part of Australia. Today's news has accounts of prominent bands and musicians decrying Reclaim Australia's use of their songs. Jimmy Barnes, John Farnham and Midnight Oil are among the artists not wanting to be associated with the hate and fear mongers. At the end of the line we walk past vertigo-inducing towers, the giant white fantasy of the Bel Air and the scruffy low-rise Tropicana with its kidney-shaped pool. Music shops are going the same way as bookshops – it's cheaper to buy the goods online – but there's a surviving store in the next block, selling highly polished violins and cellos, guitars and electric keyboards.

The Loft on Chevron Island used to be a cover-charge venue until a law change. Now they can only take donations for the musicians, and the food prices have risen. It is a tired upstairs space staffed by Asian newcomers who have kept to its original identity as Italian. There's pizza and pasta, gaudy soiled prints of Neapolitan scenes and bare-shouldered senoritas. The red carpet is thick with grime. There's a decent crowd – the locals have a special place in their hearts for this venue. First up is Hope Scott, a gifted young Gold Coast girl, then Jimmy from New Zealand who likes his guitar thrashed and his lyrics mundane. 'Cruise with the movements,' he yells, 'and create improvements.'

An ancient, drunk and unappealing Swiss takes a shine to me, and while Stan performs he bobs up and down, staring at me with a fixed grin. At the table beside the one I reluctantly share with my rictus-riven admirer a well-dressed couple in their thirties talk loudly, immune to irritated glances from the listeners. 'Could you shut up?' I ask them, eventually. The guy takes offence. It's pretty rude, he's right. I end up apologising, embarrassed, hoping Stan hasn't noticed from the stage, or even worse, his manager from the table in front. They do shut up though, listening and applauding. Later, in the bar, the talker works out that Stan is my son and apologises to me: 'He's fantastic – he should be doing ticketed events.' The techo seeks Stan out: 'Great, mate. You should see some of the people we get in here.' People shake his hand, buy copies of his band album. We float back to Brisbane on wings of praise.

25 July
Stan's manager generously lends us his car and we head to the Northern Rivers town of Bangalow to stay a couple of nights with our friend Charlie. We spend the day snooping around the country east of Lismore. The hills of Northern Rivers are familiar to me, because Tim, our youngest daughter Willa and I spent some happy months there a few years ago while Tim worked on a film. It's paradisiacal, rolling and green, planted with coffee and macadamia (the locals call it 'nut'), and stands of wet sclerophyll rainforest full of birds and pademelons.

Just outside the village of Clunes (petrol station, general store, great second-hand bookshop) we pull up short to let an echidna waddle across the road. A more impatient traveller gets out of his car and bends to the animal as if he's about to pick it up. He thinks the better of it, pulling down his sleeves to cover his luckily un-needled hands. The little marsupial takes its time – Stan and I are in no hurry.

Before he decided to follow his musical career, Stan was a science student, finishing his biology degree in marine and marsupial at Melbourne University. Echidna, he tells me, are egg-laying mammals of the monotreme order, closely related to platypus. Most often they curl up if they are frightened, but this one swaggers along with true Aussie bravado, shiny spikes wavering.

I think of Jean Devanny, the only one of my *West Island* subjects to leave New South Wales and make her home, later in life, in Townsville, Queensland. In her first (banned) novel *The Butcher Shop* (1926) she not only wrote radically about sex, race and relationships, but also wrote evocatively and lovingly about the landscape of rural New Zealand. A later novel, *Cindy*, set some 1,500 kilometres to the north of where we are now, has similar subject material – sex, race and class – and just as many loving descriptions of country. Except they are of a tropical, marginal sugar-cane plantation. I think about how when we New Zealanders fall in love with Australia we fall hard. Devanny was thirty-five when she came to live in Sydney and was never tempted to live in New Zealand again.

At the rushing, dramatic Minyon Falls, we are the only people there until a rainbow-coloured bus full of backpackers on tour from Byron Bay arrives. For half an hour or so, we have a sense of how the country was before the area got on the tourist trail and the hippies moved in. The scale is vast and the absence of human-generated noise absolute. A kookaburra calls from a dripping cedar, small green finches flit and twitter. The passengers rush to photograph the view and one of them tears a branch from a tree to toss into the void below the platform, despite signs asking him not to.

The bus is going on to Nimbin, not far away, where marijuana is openly sold on the main street and stoned kids are as common as seagulls in a rubbish dump. Northern Rivers is an area people retreat to, to find themselves, where conversations about past lives and auras and astrological signs and miraculous cures for cancer and mental illness are almost to be expected. A visit to any of the weekend markets gives a clear picture of the local tastes – organic food, fresh produce, psychics, tarot readers, and stall after stall selling muslin and velvet clothes, silver jewellery and wooden tableware. In the few months we lived here, I was as delighted with the natural beauty as much as I was depressed by a kind of spiritual emptiness that seemed to bubble up from all the soul-seeking and self-obsessed proselytising.

Our Tasmanian friend Charlie is a sensible person, more interested in facts and movies than New Age bullshit, and excellent company. A filmmaker and writer, he has lived in Bangalow with his New Zealand wife and children for fifteen years. At their house in the summer, water dragons come up the steps to the veranda, pythons curl in the trees, and last summer he was bitten by a brown snake and ended up in hospital. Brown snakes are the fourth most poisonous snake in the world and the most common cause of snakebite death in Australia, since the anti-venom can be just as toxic to certain people. There were three bites on Charlie's toe, not deep, because brown snakes have short fangs.

He tells Stan and me the story with the endearingly proud grin Australians wear when relating a story of an encounter with a snake, saltie or shark. He knew what to do – compression bandage, ring 000, wait for the paramedics. They didn't give him the shot, but he reckons it took six weeks to come right. You ache from head to foot and in some people paralysis occurs. When he was recovering, the poison affected his depth of field so that objects seemed closer or further away. I wonder if that's how snakes perceive the world and how desirable it would be to experience that state. There are hippies who smoke snake and toad poison to do just that.

A born storyteller, Charlie describes the water

dragons that live in the garden, and how the males fight for the harem of females, spreading blood everywhere but making no noise other than impact. Like most reptiles they are voiceless. I wish we could see them now as we sit on the deck in the shadowy evening with the last of the sun filtering through the Bangalow palms and gums, the small forest Charlie has planted between the house and disused railway line. But the animals are nowhere in evidence. It's mid-winter, cold enough for a layer of wool, and the reptiles are dozing.

Joke: What do you call the moron walking in shorts and bare feet through long grass? A Kiwi.

When Stan was three and we were visiting family in Oz, we went for a weekend to a friend's house outside Mudgee, about 300 kilometres north-west of Sydney, over the Blue Mountains and far, far away. It was summer, days of mead and honey and wine, sunny clear skies and a billion flies. One afternoon, when baby Maeve was having her sleep and Tim was reading, Stan and I played hide-and-seek. We hid in the woodpile, in the long grass, close to trees. When I think of it now, I can't believe I was so stupid. It wasn't as if I hadn't seen snakes in the wild in Australia (I had, once, with my trousers down, hanging constipated over a branch in the bush, a bad moment on the same holiday I saw the platypus). But for immigrants those childhood lessons aren't laid down; the fear-of-snakes instinct lies dormant. We haven't been taught what to do if we are bitten, or our mate, or our three-year-old son.

All mothers shudder if we look back at unknowing risks we took during those early years when through our own stupidity or neglect we put our children in a degree of danger – the second we turned away on the beach the toddler tumbled in the surf, the car journey home with a driver over the limit, the use of a vaccine or drug with hidden side-effects (or giving no vaccination at all), the child's outstretched hand towards the snapping dog tied to the lamp post. Playing hide-and-seek in a West Island woodpile was not too bright – but here we are, still in one piece, all these years later, together on tour.

26 July

Up early this rainy, changeable day to go to the Bangalow Market, the first time it's been able to run for five weeks. The usually dry winter has been sodden. Climate change in action. On my way out I meet Charlie coming back. He was in dire need to buy us all 'the best doughnuts in the world', but the stallholder is chasing bigger custom at a popular music festival in North Byron, Splendour in the Grass. This year they're calling it Splendour in the Mud. I wonder if it's skilly mud, which features in early Australian novels and accounts of outback life. Skilly mud is so thick and silken it can swallow a horse, and sometimes did in the days before macadam and asphalt and tarseal – the horse and the cart as well. As I cross the railway through the little forest and into the slippy market, I wonder if skilly mud still exists, treacherous enough to swallow a whole rock band.

At the market there are acres of delicious food, fresh produce and bread, the expected cotton, velvet, leather and silver, second-hand books and old china. A man I remember from three years before is still doing the exactly same act, wearing a top hat and operating a scruffy knee-high cat puppet in doublet and boots that can play the violin. Under a fig tree sits a swaying henna-haired woman in her forties, lips pursed and eyes closed in ecstasy as she pings upon her sitar. Further on, set up with guitar, amp and mike, is a Māori singer with a beautiful voice a bit like that of the late Mahinarangi Tocker. I remember the singer from when we lived here, and how one day I sat and listened and enjoyed hearing a bit of home.

In the afternoon Stan plays his last gig of this leg of the tour, three sets at a new restaurant and bar down in Byron Bay called The Farm. It's all family groups, raw wood, wide deck and courtyards. They're not used to having musicians, and set him up near the barbecue. At one stage he's enveloped in smoke but sings gamely on. Couples dance to his smoochy numbers, the kitchen staff applaud every song enthusiastically.

Afterwards an English backpacker moonlighting as a waitress says to him, 'There was a table of older people really into you.' He tells her that was his mother and her friends. 'I should've come across and had them on,' she tells him, 'said I slept with you last night and there were five other girls as well and I wasn't even jealous because you're a rock star.'

'Ah,' I say, when he tells me their banter, 'but we were up in Bangalow so I wouldn't have believed her.' Also, I think, but don't say, I brought you up to respect women. And also, more importantly, if you do ever have that much luck, I'd rather not know about it. Really.

The late lamented Celia Lashlie wrote compellingly about bringing up sons, famously telling mothers to 'get off the bridge'. She was writing about the bridge from boyhood to manhood, and how mothers must leave their sons to get on with it, to try not to boss or nag about things that are ultimately not important. I read her book when Stan was pretty much grown, and could only applaud her wisdom. Mothers and fathers tend to have divergent styles of parenting. When Stan was twelve, Tim let him walk along Karangahape Road to the Rock Shop, a famous music store on the last block before the Jewish cemetery. Being a talkative chap, he met up on the way with homeless people and prostitutes and druggies and chatted to them all. Jaunts along K Road became a regular activity from that day forth, and some of his best songs are about the people he met and got to know. If I had been bringing him up alone I would have delayed that expedition until he was about fifteen. No harm came to him on those adventures, just as it didn't in the woodpile.

27 July

Today we're heading back to Brisbane, but first we want to explore a little more. Charlie recommends the Wilson Valley. Wilson is a common name in these parts – there's Mount Wilson and the Wilson River, a tributary of the Richmond, the river that flows through Lismore and frequently floods it. In the days before railways and roads it was the main thoroughfare and the means to bring out the red cedar. Northern Rivers was once known as the Big Scrub, since it was covered in valuable timber. Red Gold they called it, as fortunes were made, until it was all gone. Less than 10 per cent of it remains, and like most logged areas of rainforest the soil is exhausted, or at least not viable enough to support a once-thriving dairy industry.

We head into the country behind the town of Mullumbimby, on a narrow dirt road slick with mud (luckily not the skilly kind). The rain has caused slips on the steep cutting. The bush reminds us of New Zealand – the pongas, or tree ferns as they call them here, a clear stream silvering mossy rocks. Bush lawyer twines around gums, supple bark swings low, isolated houses have signs on the gate warning against the proposed fracking plan for the district. Birds screech and pipe, including a wonga pigeon, which is a bird to drive you crazy. The coo resembles a car alarm – a woop, woop, woop, woop, woop – that can go on for hours. There was one that lived near us in Clunes, where I wrote *The Writing Class*, and on his rare coffee breaks I would imagine him panting with exhaustion before he started up again. I always pictured him clinging oxygen-deprived to a branch, but wongas are ground foragers, plump, with grey and white feathers, elusive and wary.

Above our heads a red escarpment rises, higher than a Gold Coast hotel, and at the end of the road beside a locked gate a sign reads 'Wanganui Walking Track Closed'. This is the trail through the Wanganui Gorge. Who called it Wanganui? Was it named after the New Zealand river valley? If I was the kind of person who believed in signs from the universe, which I'm not, I might think that we were led here by unseen forces to remind us of who we really are.

Stan went to seek his fortune in Melbourne when he was nearly twenty-one, six years ago. He has an

Australian accent now and he thinks of the West Island as home. He has a lovely sweetheart, miles of friends and all my husband's family to help him do so, not to mention his blossoming career. He is an Australian voice. Sometimes he dreams wistfully of how it would be to live in New Zealand again and in common with many expatriates it's the countryside he misses. On our way out of this remote valley he points up at an abandoned, dilapidated farmhouse, the veranda closed in for extra bedrooms. 'I could live there – no one would be bothered by my music.'

He'd last five minutes. He's an urban creature; he likes the bright lights and the crowds, the music, the arguing, the swirl and colour of human life.

We find our way back to the massive multi-lane highway to Brisbane. I'm leaving tomorrow. We don't talk much – a bit about the family and friends, his dad and his sisters, the rest of his tour. As we drive into the dusk, just the two of us, I realise I'm as happy as it's possible to be, happy and lucky in the lucky country, with the distance between my lad and me only as wide as a gearbox, not the vast Tasman Ocean.

When we say goodbye at the airport the next day, Stan's manager says, 'Now don't you cry, Mum!'

Of course I won't. I've thought a lot on this trip about how it is to have adult children, how sustaining it is to spend time with them, to click into their lives for a short time, and then go again.

Whenever I wept with loneliness during that time of adjustment to an emptier nest, my husband would say, 'We raise them to lose them.' And it's true – the most any parent can hope for their kids is independent, mostly happy, mostly fulfilling lives. And from what I've just seen, the West Island is providing that for Skyscraper Stan.

AFTERWORD

My relationship with our biggest neighbour has mostly been a very happy and fruitful one. I sometimes think that if we could take the very best attributes of both our countries and create a single nation from it – the Australian sense of humour, our greater respect for the indigenous, the Australian confidence and bravado, our politeness, reticence and concern for the environment – it would be a very fine nation indeed. It is not an idea I would ever want to see made real, more an idea that could inspire a novel or a film. The plot would spin around a civil war as true New Zealanders rebel against losing their sovereignty and sense of self, just as we have done in the face of the Trans Pacific Partnership.

Even so, if I was to learn today that I would never visit the West Island again, I would feel as though

I had lost a part of my heart. I can feel almost as at home there as I do here, a conviction so common among New Zealanders as to be almost be a national characteristic.

I'll leave you with a scene that I imagine has played out in one version or other in thousands of trans-Tasman families. When Stan was born at the Royal Women's Hospital in Paddington, my parents were visiting Sydney. Stan was the first grandchild on either side. I wrote this poem for his twenty-first birthday in 2009.

On the Occasion of His Twenty-first Birthday

When first I held you in my arms
the feminist dissolved.
'My son!' We had a lad, a little
bloke, a chappie, a fella, a cove.

'He'll play for the Wallabies' said Woody
'The All Blacks you mean' said Dad
'He'll be the first bloke who plays for them
  both' the grandads
said, as they stood around the bed.

When I first held you in my arms
I wished for you a life
of love, adventure, brave ideas,
beauty, philosophy, an absence of fear –

And here you are this mid-winter night
more splendid than I could have imagined.
Bluesman, marineman,
domestic disaster,

joker, poet, brother of two sisters,
charmer, mentor, our golden son
flying from these islands
now you are twenty-one.

We toast you and farewell you,
our giant among men.

(And he does play for both countries, very well, but not rugby.)

NOTES

1 Carole Ferrier (ed.), *Point of Departure: The Autobiography of Jean Devanny*, University of Queensland Press, St Lucia, 1986.

2 Clement Semmler, *Douglas Stewart*, Twayne Publishers Inc., New York, 1974.

3 The inquest found he had taken LSD for the first time that day and was hallucinating when he fell from the cliff.

4 In the first week of my return the decision was made to allow the New Zealand police force to carry Tasers.

5 Leslie Walton, *The Art of Roland Wakelin*, Craftsman House, Seaforth, NSW, 1987.

ABOUT THE AUTHOR

Stephanie Johnson is a leading New Zealand novelist whose books have won many awards. Her novel *The Shag Incident* won the Montana Deutz Medal for Fiction in 2003. Her most recent novels have been *The Writing Class* and *The Writers' Festival.* She has published collections of poetry, short stories and plays, and worked as an actress. She is also a critic and creative writing teacher.

About BWB Texts

BWB Texts are short books on big subjects: succinct narratives spanning history, memoir, contemporary issues, science and more from great New Zealand writers. All BWB Texts are available digitally, with selected works also in paperback. New Texts are published monthly – visit www.bwb.co.nz to see the latest releases.

BWB Texts include:

Paul Callaghan: Luminous Moments
Foreword by Catherine Callaghan

Creeks and Kitchens: A Childhood Memoir
Maurice Gee

Report from Christchurch
Rebecca Macfie

'I think ... I am going to die.': Katherine Mansfield at Fontainebleau
Kathleen Jones

Geering and God, 1965–71: The Heresy Trial that Divided New Zealand
Lloyd Geering

Inequality and the West
Robert Wade

The Zealandia Drowning Debate: Did New Zealand Sink Beneath the Waves?
Hamish Campbell

The Quiet War on Asylum
Tracey Barnett

What Happened at Waitangi?
Claudia Orange

When the Tour Came to Auckland
Geoff Chapple

Thorndon: Wellington and Home: My Katherine Mansfield Project
Kirsty Gunn

The Inequality Debate: An Introduction
Max Rashbroo

First Contact: Tasman's Arrival in Taitapu, 1642
Anne Salmond

Wellbeing Economics: Future Directions for New Zealand
Paul Dalziel & Caroline Saunders

Growing Apart: Regional Prosperity in New Zealand
Shamubeel Eaqub

Parihaka Invaded
Dick Scott

Barefoot Years
Martin Edmond

The Piketty Phenomenon: New Zealand Perspectives
Various

Bombing the Rainbow Warrior: The Intimate Story of Two French Agents and the New Zealand Police
Michael King

Samoa mo Samoa: Black Saturday 1929
Michael Field

Tunes for Bears to Dance To: The Shaping of a New Zealand Writer
Owen Marshall

The Child Poverty Debate: Myths, Misconceptions and Misunderstandings
Jonathan Boston & Simon Chapple

The Struggle for Sovereignty: New Zealand and Twenty-First Century Statehood
Margaret Wilson

Ruth, Roger and Me: Debts and Legacies
Andrew Dean

On Coming Home
Paula Morris

Haerenga: Early Māori Journeys Across the Globe
Vincent O'Malley

Generation Rent: Rethinking New Zealand's Priorities
Shamubeel & Selena Eaqub

No Country for Old Maids? Talking About the 'Man Drought'
Hannah August

Time of Useful Consciousness: Acting Urgently on Climate Change
Ralph Chapman

Out of the Vaipe, the Deadwater: A Writer's Early Life
Albert Wendt

Polluted Inheritance: New Zealand's Freshwater Crisis
Mike Joy

Wealth and New Zealand
Max Rashbrooke

Why Science Is Sexist
Nicola Gaston

Christchurch Ruptures
Katie Pickles

The Interregnum: Rethinking New Zealand
Morgan Godfery (ed)

Going Places: Migration, Economics and the Future of New Zealand
Julie Fry & Hayden Glass

Silencing Science
Shaun Hendy

The First Migration: Māori Origins 3000BC – AD1450
Atholl Anderson